BORDER CROSSINGS

Sneed B. Collard III

Illustrated by Howard Gray

Charlesbridge

For my son, Braden, who crosses la frontera with me.
Love, Daddy—S. B. C. III

For my daughters, Rowan and Kes, who always
inspire me—H. G.

Text copyright © 2023 by Sneed B. Collard III
Illustrations copyright © 2023 by Howard Gray
All rights reserved, including the right of reproduction
   in whole or in part in any form. Charlesbridge and
   colophon are registered trademarks of Charlesbridge
   Publishing, Inc.

At the time of publication, all URLs printed in this book
were accurate and active. Charlesbridge, the author,
and the illustrator are not responsible for the content
or accessibility of any website.

Published by Charlesbridge
9 Galen Street
Watertown, MA 02472
(617) 926-0329
www.charlesbridge.com

Printed in China
(hc) 10 9 8 7 6 5 4 3 2 1

Illustrations done in digital media
Display type set in Woolwich Eroded Regular
   by David Kerkhoff
Text type set in Unna by Jorge de Buen Unna and
   Avenir by Adrian Frutiger
Printed by 1010 Printing International Limited in
   Huizhou, Guangdong, China
Production supervision by Mira Kennedy
Designed by Jon Simeon

Library of Congress Cataloging-in-Publication Data
Names: Collard, Sneed B., author. | Gray, Howard, illustrator.
Title: Border crossings / by Sneed B. Collard III; illustrated by
   Howard Gray.
Description: Watertown, MA: Charlesbridge Publishing, 2023. |
   Includes bibliographical references. | Audience: Ages 6–9. |
   Audience: Grades 2–3. | Summary: "As two ocelots attempt to
   cross the United States-Mexico border, they face obstacles that
   drive home the catastrophic effects of a wall on the plants and
   animals of the border—and the many benefits of keeping the
   border barrier-free."—Provided by publisher.
Identifiers: LCCN 2020028056 (print) | LCCN 2020028057 (ebook) |
   ISBN 9781623542382 (hardcover) | ISBN 9781632896087 (ebook)
Subjects: LCSH: Ocelot—Effect of human beings on—Mexican-
   American Border Region—Juvenile literature. | Border crossing—
   Mexican-American Border Region—Juvenile literature. |
   Boundaries—Environmental aspects—Mexican-American Border
   Region—Juvenile literature.
Classification: LCC QL737.C23 C647 2023 (print) |
   LCC QL737.C23 (ebook) | DDC 599.75/2—dc23
LC record available at https://lccn.loc.gov/2020028056
LC ebook record available at https://lccn.loc.gov/2020028057

On a moonless night, padded paws silently step across pebbled ground. They make their way past thorn trees, through brush, and around a muddy marsh. They halt, alert and tense. Then they continue walking.

The paws belong to a young ocelot, one of the rarest animals in the United States. It is springtime, and the beautifully spotted male cat is heading south, toward Mexico, looking for a mate and a territory he can call his own.

The ocelot's movements are cloaked by thick brush and the cover of darkness. But suddenly he encounters something unexpected. Something frightening.

Where protective plants once stood, an ugly scar now stretches.

Running in both directions, as far as the ocelot can see, looms a wall.

The ocelot has encountered fences and ditches before
but nothing like this. Cautiously, he creeps across the
wide expanse and up to the tall, strange structure.
He sniffs at the gleaming metal. The wall smells
alien. Out of place.

The ocelot places a paw on the structure. He is a
good climber, but his claws slide uselessly on the
wall's metal surface.

He tries to squeeze through the wall, but the gaps are too narrow. He is searching for a way around the wall or under it when . . .

harsh headlights approach,   accompanied by a loud roaring sound.

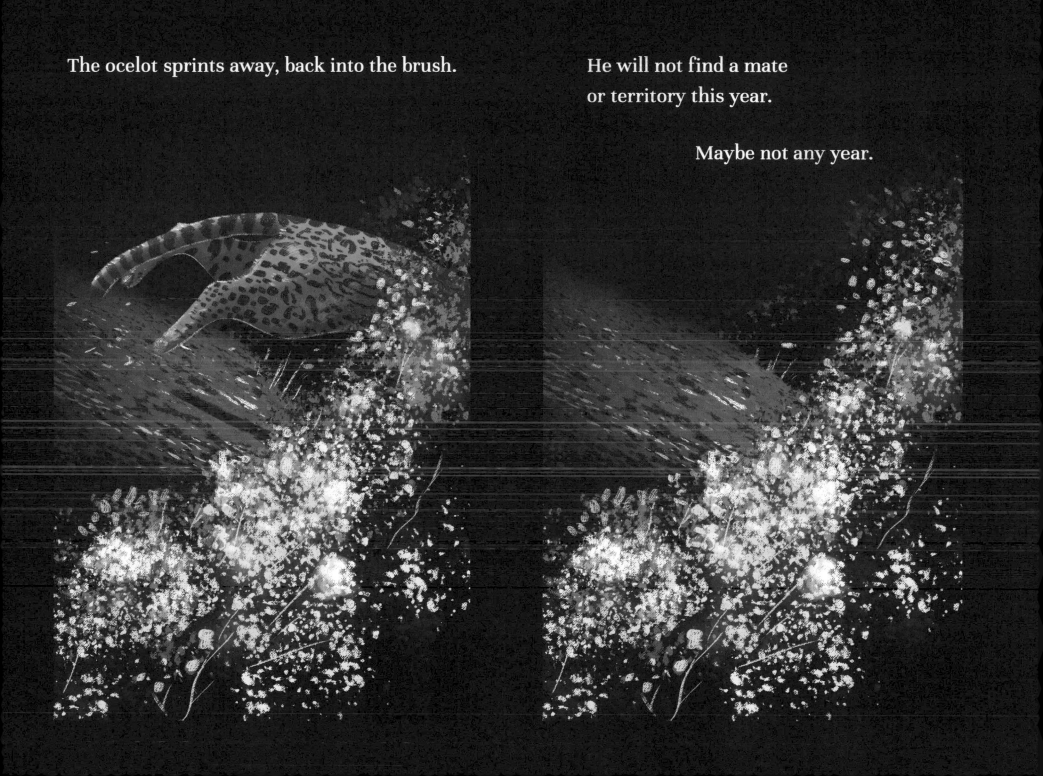

The ocelot sprints away, back into the brush.

He will not find a mate
or territory this year.

Maybe not any year.

The ocelot has been turned back by the border wall. The border is a line created to separate two great nations, the United States and Mexico.

For the ocelot and other animals, however, these aren't separate lands. They are connected by some of the richest habitats in North America.

The border stretches almost two thousand miles from the Pacific Ocean to the Gulf of Mexico. It runs through chaparral and desert. Mountain and canyon.

It cuts through forest, grassland, and brushlands that are home to many plants and animals found nowhere else on Earth.

Night and day, countless animals cross and recross the border. In the Sonoran Desert, a thousand miles from the male ocelot, a group of javelinas forages for juicy leaves and fruits.

Rare Sonoran pronghorn stop for a drink at a precious watering hole. Warblers and other songbirds fill up on insects and fruits to fuel their migrations north.

Come nightfall, a female ocelot also is on the move.
She follows canyons and arroyos north through the dark
desert. In places, saguaro cactuses tower over her.
Prickly cholla and barrel cactuses crouch in between.

The cat hears the stalks of willowy ocotillo plants scratching against one another in the breeze. She smells the sweet scent of their blood-red blooms.

Like the male ocelot, the female ocelot reaches the United States-Mexico border. Here she finds no barrier to stop her. The desert stretches without a break, connecting the two countries, not dividing them.

The ocelot can continue north, searching for a fresh territory to live in. One with food, water—maybe even another ocelot.

The animals and plants of the border have inhabited and passed through this region for thousands of years.

They adapted to changing climates.

They witnessed the arrival of the earliest humans. They moved freely back and forth across the land—long before there were countries.

Long before there was a thing called the border.

But today, the border wall threatens these animals'
survival. Some can fly over the wall or find their
way through it.

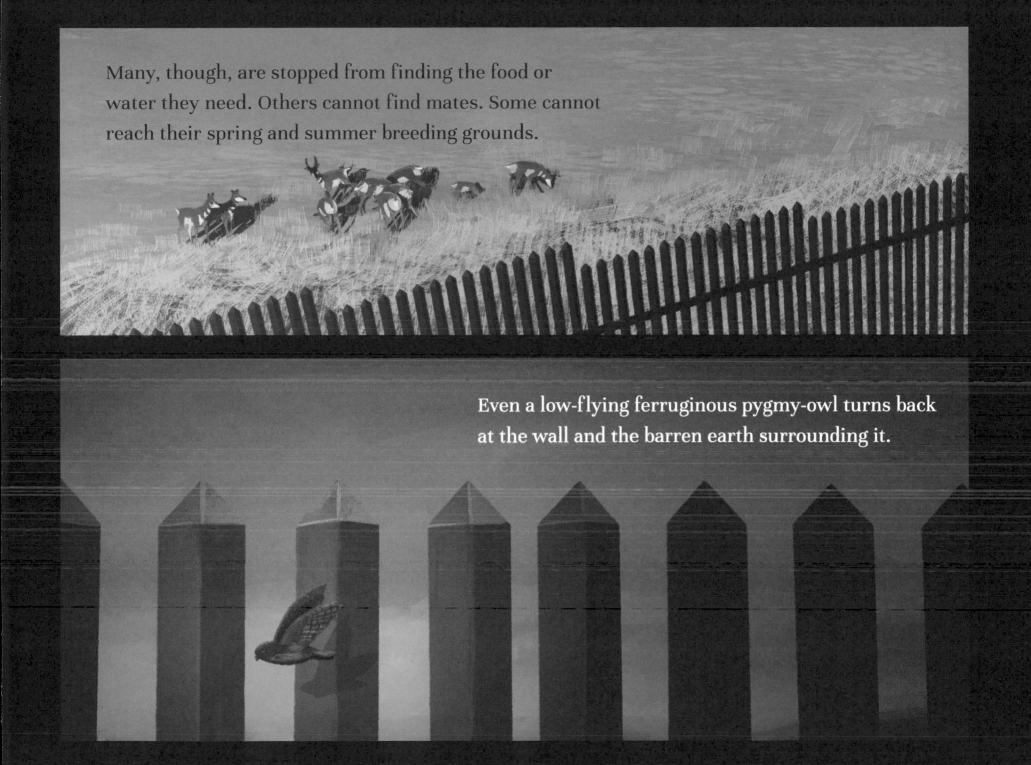

Many, though, are stopped from finding the food or water they need. Others cannot find mates. Some cannot reach their spring and summer breeding grounds.

Even a low-flying ferruginous pygmy-owl turns back at the wall and the barren earth surrounding it.

Fortunately, the wall is not everywhere. Not yet.

In places, animals still move freely about this spectacular region. They cross the made-up line that humans have created.

For them the border is not something that separates. It is something that connects. For them the border is quite simply . . .

Home.

AUTHOR'S NOTE

The United States-Mexico border stretches just under two thousand miles from San Diego, California, to Brownsville, Texas. Many people think of this area as a wasteland, but the border is one of the richest places in North America for plants and animals. It is home to at least six major ecosystems, each with its own special community of life. The Chihuahuan Desert alone has one thousand kinds of plants found nowhere else on Earth.

At least seven hundred kinds of birds, mammals, and insects pass through the border area as they migrate north and south every year. Many more animals make the borderlands their permanent homes. The border region is the only place in the United States where you can find ocelots, jaguars, gray hawks, and aplomado falcons. It is the only home for juniper titmice and black-tailed prairie dogs in Mexico. Animals such as the endangered Sonoran pronghorn live in the border region of both countries.

Human activities have greatly impacted animals and plants along the border. Dams, roads, farming, cattle grazing, pollution, pesticides, and the spread of invasive species have harmed the endangered desert pupfish, narrow-headed garter snake, Chiricahua leopard frog, and many other animals. Hotter temperatures and drier conditions from climate change are also hurting wildlife. Sprawling cities on both sides of the border gobble up habitat and block corridors that animals such as ocelots need to reach each other.

The construction of the border wall looms as yet another threat. Hundreds of miles of the wall already have been built, and as of this writing, new construction continues. The wall is designed to keep people from coming to the United States illegally—often to escape violence where they live or to find higher-paying jobs. But desperate people continue to find ways to climb, cut through, or dig under the wall. They often end up in harsh desert areas, where many die from exposure and dehydration. The wall also separates communities, including many families, that have freely interacted across the border for generations. Beyond this human toll, the wall stops the movement of many animals.

Only about fifty ocelots live in the United States. These cats live mainly in Texas. They have also been recently sighted in Arizona. For these tiny populations to keep healthy, they must be able to interact and breed with ocelots living on the Mexican side of the border. Cut off from Mexico, they will become inbred and, perhaps, fail to find mates. Wildlife workers have discussed bringing Mexican ocelots to Texas or taking Texan ocelots to Mexico, but a better long-term solution would be to make sure a wildlife corridor stays open, allowing the cats to move freely. The wall would block this corridor.

In Arizona, large sections of the border remained "wall free" when I first wrote this book. That's why I showed the second ocelot crossing the border in the desert. Since then, the wall has been installed along most of the Arizona border, making it less likely that ocelots will ever establish a larger presence there or interact with neighboring ocelots in Mexico.

The actual barrier isn't the only problem. Engineers often scrape a wide barren strip on both sides of a border wall. This destroys thousands of acres of habitat that plants and animals need. Many animals—even if they can squeeze through the openings in a wall—won't cross the empty strips of dirt surrounding it.

Walls do not have to be permanent, however, and prominent gaps and other features can be added or maintained to help wildlife. A number of groups, including the Center for Biological Diversity (www.biologicaldiversity.org) and Defenders of Wildlife (www.defenders.org), are working to protect fragile border ecosystems. If you care about the border region and its plants and animals, read some of the books listed on the next page and search online for more information. You also can share your thoughts about the border by writing to your representatives and senators in Congress— and to the President of the United States. The border region is one of the world's great natural treasures, but there is only one way to protect it: by letting others know that we care.

GLOSSARY

chaparral: A drought-resistant ecosystem dominated by scrubby, highly flammable plants.

border: The human-made line separating two nations, in this case the United States and Mexico.

breeding: Mating and having young.

climate change: The heating up of our planet due to rising levels of carbon dioxide and other gases in Earth's atmosphere.

ecosystem: A community of animals, plants, and other living things that live and function together. Examples include rain forests, coral reefs, and deserts.

endangered: Close to extinction. A living thing that is endangered may soon disappear from Earth forever.

habitat: A place that is home to plants, animals, and other living things.

inbred: A condition that occurs when there is not enough variation in breeding individuals. Inbreeding can lead to weaker animals with more diseases and health problems.

migration: The usually predictable or seasonal movement of animals to reach food, breeding areas, or other resources.

threatened: Close to becoming endangered.

FURTHER READING

Several children's books offer insights into the struggles of immigrants and the human costs of border walls. These stories can be difficult to read, but they can also lead to important discussions about borders, immigration, and our shared humanity.

Areli Is a Dreamer: A True Story by Areli Morales (Random House Studio, 2021)

Bright Star by Yuyi Morales (Neal Porter Books, 2021)

La Frontera: El viaje con papá/My Journey with Papa by Deborah Mills and Alfredo Alva (Barefoot Books, 2018)

My Two Border Towns by David Bowles (Kokila, 2021)

Pancho Rabbit and the Coyote: A Migrant's Tale by Duncan Tonatiuh (Abrams, 2013)

Almost nothing has been published that explores the toll of border walls on wildlife and ecosystems. To learn more, search online for "environmental impacts of border wall," and a number of excellent articles will come up. Check your library for these books about ocelots and desert ecosystems:

Desert Days, Desert Nights by Roxie Munro (Bright Sky Press, 2010)

Desert Food Webs in Action by Paul Fleisher (Lerner, 2014)

Desert Night Desert Day by Anthony D. Fredericks (Rio Chico, 2011)

Javelinas by Conrad J. Storad (Lerner Publications, 2008)

Many Biomes, One Earth by Sneed B. Collard III (Charlesbridge, 2009)

Ocelots by Henry Randall (Powerkids Press, 2011)

Sonoran Desert by Wayne Lynch (NorthWord, 2009)

Welcome to the Desert by Honor Head (Ruby Tuesday Books, 2017)

Teachers, parents, and guardians: The excellent PG-13 film *The River and the Wall* (2019) documents environmental, economic, and social aspects of the US-Mexico border and implications of a border wall.